RICKY RICOTTA'S

# MIGHTY ROBOT

STORY BY

DAV PILKEY

ART BY

DAN SANTAT

SCHOLASTIC INC.

**FOR MIGHTY MEENA AND HER BEST BUDDY, NITRO NIKHIL**

**– D.P.**

**FOR ALEK AND KYLE – TWO BROTHERS, AND BEST OF FRIENDS**

**– D.S.**



Library of Congress Cataloging-in-Publication Data

Pilkey, Dav, 1966 – author.
Ricky Ricotta's mighty robot / story by Dav Pilkey ; art by Dan Santat. — Revised edition.
pages cm
Summary: Ricky Ricotta, a small mouse, is being bullied at school, but when he rescues a powerful robot from its evil creator, he acquires a friend and protector — and saves the city from Dr. Stinky.
1. Mice — Juvenile fiction. 2. Robots — Juvenile fiction. 3. Bullying — Juvenile fiction. 4. Heroes — Juvenile fiction. [1. Mice — Fiction. 2. Robots — Fiction 3. Bullying — Fiction. 4. Heroes — Fiction.] I. Santat, Dan, illustrator. II. Title.
PZ7.P63123Ro 2014 813.54 — dc23 2013050798

ISBN 978-93-5103-224-3

Printed in India at Sai Printo Pack Pvt. Ltd.

First printing, May 2014
This reprint edition, February 2026

Book design by Phil Falco

# CHAPTERS

# CHAPTER ONE
# RICKY

There once was a mouse named Ricky Ricotta who lived in Squeakyville with his mother and father.

Ricky liked living with his mother and father, but sometimes he got lonely.

Ricky wished he had a friend to keep him company.

"Don't worry," said Ricky's father. "Someday something **BIG** will happen, and you will find a friend."

So Ricky waited.

## CHAPTER TWO
# THE BULLIES

Ricky liked school, but he did not like walking to school. This was because Ricky was very small, and sometimes bullies picked on him.

"Where do you think you are going?" asked one of the bullies.

Ricky did not answer. He turned and started to run.

The bullies chased him.

They knocked Ricky down and threw his backpack into a garbage can.

Every day, the bullies chased Ricky.

Every day, they knocked him down.

And every day, Ricky wished that something **BIG** would happen.

## CHAPTER THREE
# DR. STINKY McNASTY

That day at school, Ricky ate lunch by himself. Then he went outside for recess.

He watched the other mice play a game of kickball. Ricky did not know that something **BIG** was about to happen, but it *was*!

In a secret cave above the city, a mad doctor was planning something evil.

Dr. Stinky McNasty had created a Mighty Robot.

"I will use this Robot to destroy the city," said Dr. Stinky, "and soon, I will rule the world!"

Dr. Stinky led his Mighty Robot into town.

"Robot," said Dr. Stinky, "let's have some fun!"

# CHAPTER FOUR
# THE MIGHTY ROBOT

BOOM
BOOM
BOOM
HUH?
BOOM
BOOM
HA! HA! HA!
JUMP, ROBOT! JUMP!

BOING
CRASH
YAAAA!
EEEEK!
RUN AWAY!

VERY GOOD.
NOW STOMP, ROBOT, STOMP!

CRASH
CRASH
CRASH
HAW!
HAW!
HAW!

EVEN
BETTER!

NOW DESTROY
THIS CITY!

?
YOU HEARD ME!!!
DESTROY THIS CITY... OR I'LL DESTROY YOU!

THE MIGHTY ROBOT LOOKED AROUND.

HE SAW THE INNOCENT MICE...

...HE SAW THE FRIGHTENED CHILDREN...

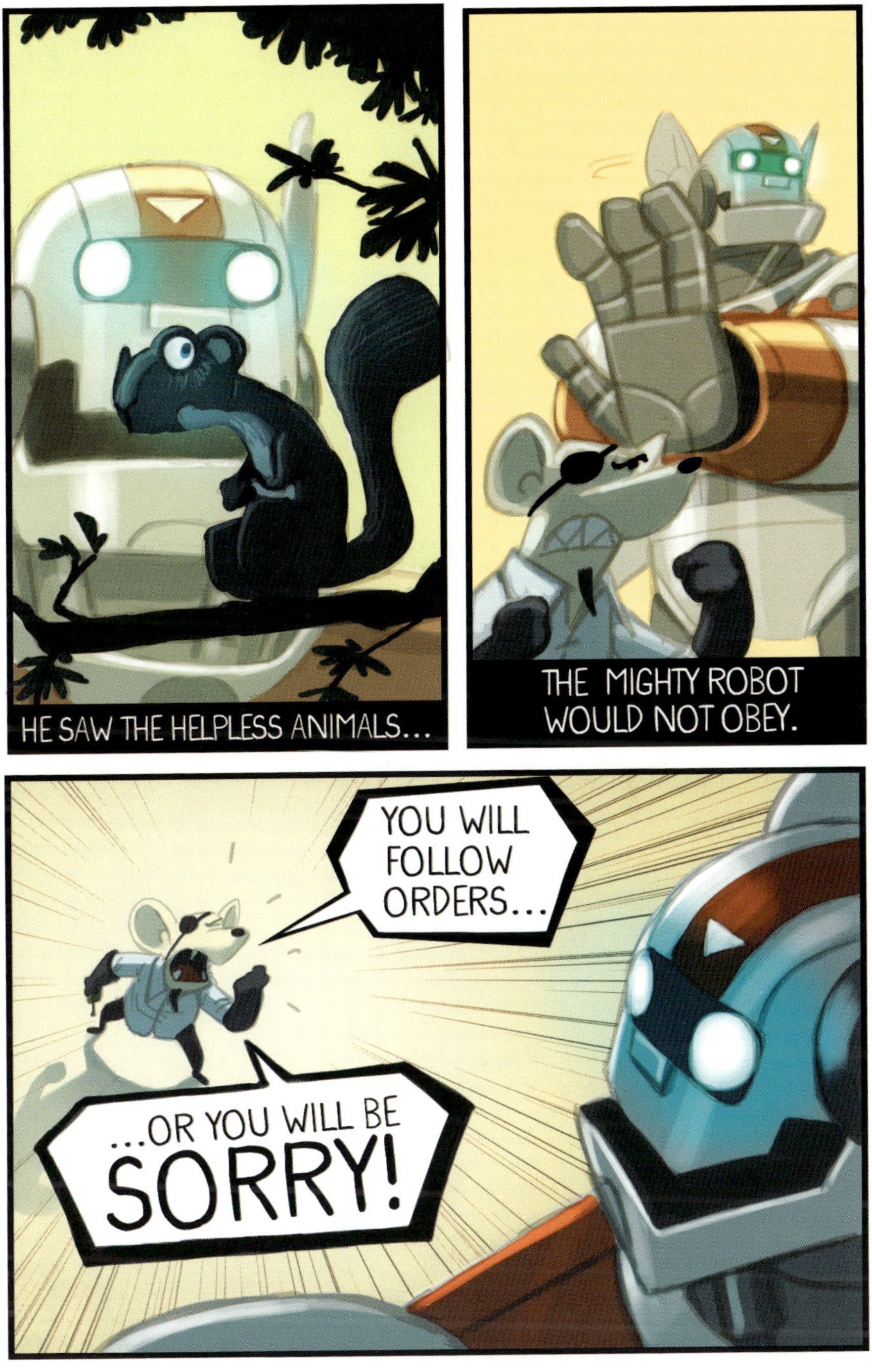
HE SAW THE HELPLESS ANIMALS...
THE MIGHTY ROBOT WOULD NOT OBEY.
YOU WILL FOLLOW ORDERS...
...OR YOU WILL BE SORRY!

## CHAPTER FIVE
# RICKY TO THE RESCUE

Dr. Stinky was very angry.

"Destroy Squeakyville!" he cried. "Destroy Squeakyville!" But the Robot refused.

"I will teach you a lesson," said Dr. Stinky. He pressed a button on his remote control and zapped the Robot with a terrible shock.

Ricky was watching.

"Stop it!" Ricky cried. But Dr. Stinky kept on zapping the Robot.

Finally, Ricky aimed a kickball at the evil doctor. Ricky kicked as hard as he could.

*BOING!* The kickball bounced off Dr. Stinky's head. Dr. Stinky dropped the controller, and it broke on the ground.

“Rats! Rats! *RATS!*” cried Dr. Stinky. “I shall return!” And he disappeared down a sewer drain.

When the Robot saw what Ricky had done, he walked over to Ricky. Everyone screamed and ran.

But Ricky was not afraid. The Robot smiled and patted Ricky on the head.

Something **BIG** had happened after all!

## CHAPTER SIX
# THE HEROES ARRIVE

That afternoon, the Robot followed Ricky home from school.

Soon they got to Ricky's house.
"Wait here, Robot," said Ricky.
Ricky went inside.

"Mom, Dad," said Ricky, "can I have a pet?"

"Well," said Ricky's father, "you've been a good mouse lately."

"Yes," said Ricky's mother, "I think a pet would be good for you."

"Hooray!" said Ricky.
"Uh-oh," said Ricky's parents.

## CHAPTER SEVEN

# RICKY'S MIGHTY ROBOT HELPS OUT

When Ricky's parents saw Ricky's new pet, they were not happy.

"That Robot is too big to be a pet," said Ricky's father.

"There is no room for him in our home," said Ricky's mom.

“But he is my friend,” said Ricky, “and he will help us around the house!”

Ricky's Mighty Robot used his super breath to blow all the leaves out of their yard. Ricky's dad liked that.

Ricky's Robot scared all the crows out of the vegetable garden. Ricky's mom liked that.

And when burglars drove by the Ricottas' house, they kept right on driving. Everybody liked that!

"Well," said Ricky's father, "I guess your Robot can live in the garage."

"Hooray!" said Ricky.

## CHAPTER EIGHT
# BACK TO SCHOOL

The next day, Ricky and his Robot walked to school. The bullies were waiting for Ricky.

"Where do you think you're going?" asked one of the bullies.

“My Robot and I are going to school,” said Ricky.

The bullies looked up and saw Ricky’s Mighty Robot. They were very frightened.

"Um . . . um . . . um . . ." said one of the bullies. "May we carry your backpack for you, sir?"

"Sure," said Ricky.

The bullies helped Ricky get to school safely.

"Is there anything else we can do for you, sir?" asked the bullies.

"No, thank you," said Ricky.

## CHAPTER NINE
# SHOW-AND-TELL

That day at school, Ricky's class had show-and-tell. One mouse brought a baseball glove. Another mouse brought a teddy bear.

Ricky brought his Mighty Robot.

Ricky's class got a free ride on the Robot's back.

They flew up above the
city and over the mountains.

"This is fun!" said Ricky.

# CHAPTER TEN
# DR. STINKY'S REVENGE

While Ricky's class was flying around in the sky, Dr. Stinky sneaked over to the school. He wanted revenge!

Dr. Stinky crept into Ricky's classroom. He saw their pet lizard.

"This is just what I need!" said Dr. Stinky.

He took out a bottle of Hate Potion #9 and put a drop into the lizard's water dish. The lizard drank the water.

Suddenly, the lizard began to grow and change. He got bigger and bigger. He got meaner and meaner.

Soon, the lizard turned into an evil monster.

"Destroy Ricky and his Robot!" said Dr. Stinky.

"Yes, Master!" said the monster.

When Ricky's Robot saw the evil monster, he flew down to the school yard. Ricky and his class climbed off quickly. Then, the Robot turned toward the giant creature, and the battle began.

# CHAPTER ELEVEN
# THE BIG BATTLE

ROAAR!
SHOOOOF

CRASH!
NOOOOO!
GO GET HIM, BUDDY!

FOOOOOOSH!
SLAM!

THWIP!
CRACK
*CHOKE*
SPLASH

SCREEEEEECH!
*HUFF*HUFF*HUFF*
MIGHTY ROBOT!
*GLURK*
*GLURK*
*GLURK*
MIGHTY ROBOT!!

FWOOSH

CRASH!

## CHAPTER TWELVE

# THE FINAL BATTLE

## (IN FLIP-O-RAMA™)

FLIP-O
HEY, KIDS! YOU CAN ANIMATE THE ACTION BY FOLLOWING THESE EASY STEPS!

# -RAMA

## HERE'S HOW IT WORKS!

### STEP 1

Place your *left* hand inside the dotted lines marked "LEFT HAND HERE." Hold the book open *flat*.

### STEP 2

Grasp the *right-hand* page with your right thumb and index finger (inside the dotted lines marked "RIGHT THUMB HERE").

### STEP 3

Now *quickly* flip the right-hand page back and forth until the picture appears to be *animated*.

(For extra fun, try adding your own sound-effects!)

# FLIP-O-RAMA 1

(pages 77 and 79)

Remember, flip *only* page 77.
While you are flipping, be sure you
can see the picture on page 77
*and* the one on page 79.
If you flip quickly, the two
pictures will start to look like
<u>one</u> *animated* picture.

Don't forget to add
your own sound-effects!

LEFT HAND HERE

THE MONSTER ATTACKED.

RIGHT THUMB HERE

RIGHT
INDEX
FINGER
HERE

**THE MONSTER ATTACKED.**

# FLIP-O-RAMA 2

(pages 81 and 83)

Remember, flip *only* page 81.
While you are flipping, be sure you can see the picture on page 81 *and* the one on page 83.
If you flip quickly, the two pictures will start to look like one *animated* picture.

Don't forget to add your own sound-effects!

LEFT HAND HERE

RICKY'S ROBOT
FOUGHT BACK.

RIGHT
THUMB
HERE

RIGHT
INDEX
FINGER
HERE

RICKY'S ROBOT FOUGHT BACK.

# FLIP-O-RAMA 3

(pages 85 and 87)

Remember, flip *only* page 85.
While you are flipping, be sure you can see the picture on page 85 *and* the one on page 87.
If you flip quickly, the two pictures will start to look like one *animated* picture.

Don't forget to add your own sound-effects!

LEFT HAND HERE

THE MONSTER
BATTLED HARD.

RIGHT
THUMP
HERE

RIGHT
INDEX
FINGER
HERE

**THE MONSTER BATTLED HARD.**

# FLIP-O-RAMA 4

(pages 89 and 91)

Remember, flip *only* page 89.
While you are flipping, be sure you
can see the picture on page 89
*and* the one on page 91.
If you flip quickly, the two
pictures will start to look like
<u>one</u> *animated* picture.

Don't forget to add
your own sound-effects!

LEFT HAND HERE

**RICKY'S ROBOT BATTLED HARDER.**

RIGHT THUMB HERE

RIGHT
INDEX
FINGER
HERE

RICKY'S ROBOT
BATTLED HARDER.

# FLIP-O-RAMA 5

(pages 93 and 95)

Remember, flip *only* page 93.
While you are flipping, be sure you can see the picture on page 93 *and* the one on page 95.
If you flip quickly, the two pictures will start to look like one *animated* picture.

Don't forget to add your own sound-effects!

LEFT HAND HERE

RICKY'S ROBOT SAVED THE DAY.

RIGHT THUMB HERE

RIGHT
INDEX
FINGER
HERE

RICKY'S ROBOT
SAVED THE DAY.

## CHAPTER THIRTEEN
# THE ELECTRO-ROCKET

The monster was defeated, and all of his evil powers went away. Soon, he turned back into a tiny lizard and never bothered anybody again.

"Rats! Rats! *RATS!*" cried Dr. Stinky. "I will destroy that Robot myself!" He took his Electro-Rocket and aimed it at Ricky's Robot.

“NO!” screamed Ricky. He leaped onto Dr. Stinky just as the evil doctor fired his rocket.

Up, up, up went the rocket. Ricky's Robot flew after it. But he was not fast enough.

The rocket came down and exploded.

***Ka-BOOM!***

Right on Dr. Stinky's secret cave.

## CHAPTER FOURTEEN
# JUSTICE PREVAILS

"Rats! Rats! *RATS!*" cried Dr. Stinky. "This has been a bad day for me!"

"It is about to get worse," said Ricky.

Ricky's Mighty Robot picked up Dr. Stinky and put him in the city jail.

# CHAPTER FIFTEEN
# BACK HOME

That night, the Ricotta family had a cookout in the backyard. Ricky told his mom and dad all about their adventures that day.

"Thank you for saving the city," said Ricky's father.

"And thank you for saving each other," said Ricky's mother.

"No problem," said Ricky . . .

. . . "that's what friends are for."

# MORE RICKY?

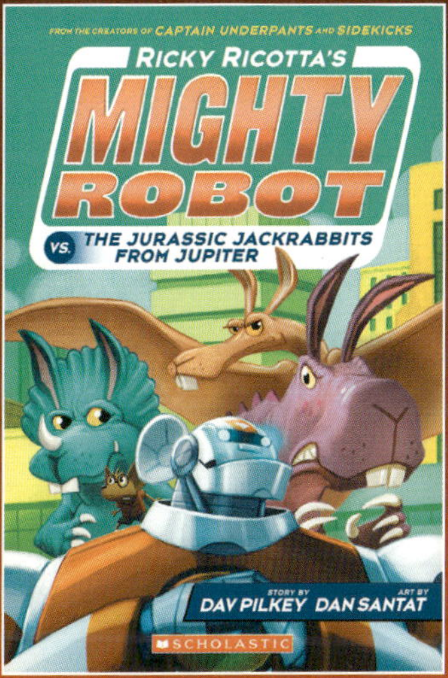
FROM THE CREATORS OF CAPTAIN UNDERPANTS AND SIDEKICKS
RICKY RICOTTA'S
MIGHTY ROBOT
VS. THE JURASSIC JACKRABBITS FROM JUPITER
STORY BY DAV PILKEY
ART BY DAN SANTAT
SCHOLASTIC

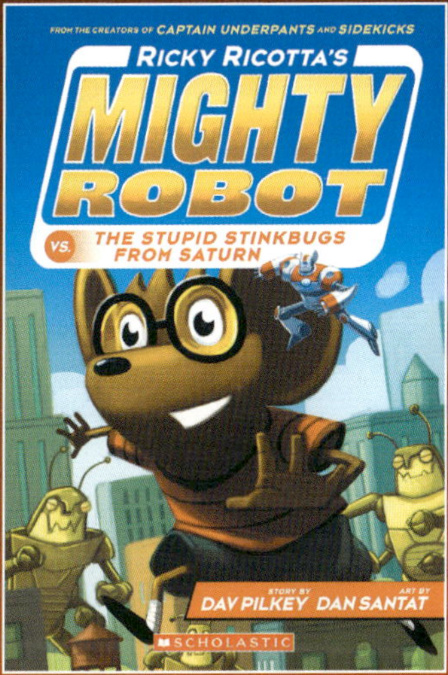
FROM THE CREATORS OF CAPTAIN UNDERPANTS AND SIDEKICKS
RICKY RICOTTA'S
MIGHTY ROBOT
VS. THE STUPID STINKBUGS FROM SATURN
STORY BY DAV PILKEY
ART BY DAN SANTAT
SCHOLASTIC

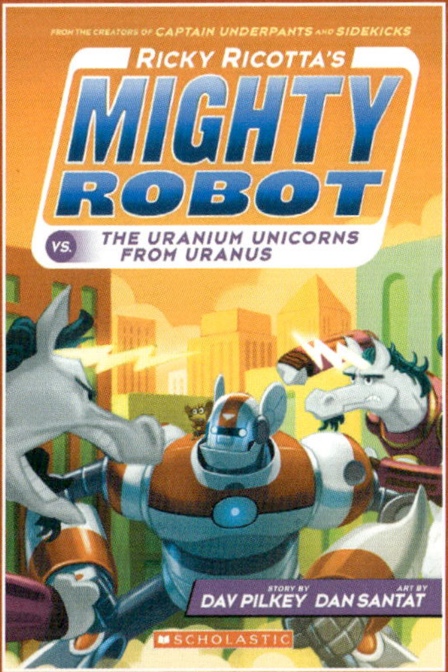
FROM THE CREATORS OF CAPTAIN UNDERPANTS AND SIDEKICKS
RICKY RICOTTA'S
MIGHTY ROBOT
VS. THE URANIUM UNICORNS FROM URANUS
STORY BY DAV PILKEY
ART BY DAN SANTAT
SCHOLASTIC

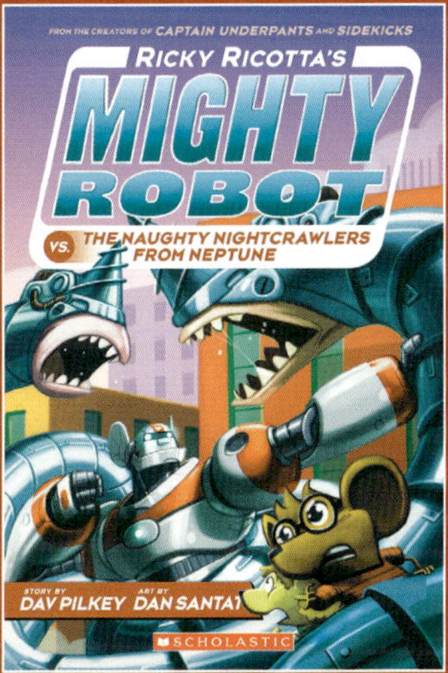
FROM THE CREATORS OF CAPTAIN UNDERPANTS AND SIDEKICKS
RICKY RICOTTA'S
MIGHTY ROBOT
VS. THE NAUGHTY NIGHTCRAWLERS FROM NEPTUNE
STORY BY DAV PILKEY
ART BY DAN SANTAT
SCHOLASTIC

## DAV PILKEY

has written and illustrated more than fifty books for children, including *The Paperboy*, a Caldecott Honor book; *Dog Breath: The Horrible Trouble with Hally Tosis*, winner of the California Young Reader Medal; and the IRA Children's Choice Dumb Bunnies series. He is also the creator of the *New York Times* best-selling Captain Underpants books. Dav lives in the Pacific Northwest with his wife. Find him online at www.pilkey.com.

## DAN SANTAT

is the writer and illustrator of the picture book *The Adventures of Beekle: The Unimaginary Friend*. He is also the creator of the graphic novel *Sidekicks* and has illustrated many acclaimed picture books, including the *New York Times* bestseller *Because I'm Your Dad* by Ahmet Zappa and *Crankenstein* by Samantha Berger. Dan also created the Disney animated hit *The Replacements*. He lives in Southern California with his family. Find him online at www.dantat.com.